The Wild Life of Pets

A RUBES® CARTOON BOOK

BY LEIGH RUBIN

BOWTIE PRESS

IRVINE, CALIFORNIA

For Teresa, Jeremy, Ryan, Andrew, and Willie

Ruth Strother, Project Manager
Nick Clemente, Special Consultant
Michelle Martinez, Editor
Karla Austin, Associate Editor
Michael Vincent Capozzi, Designer

Library of Congress Control Number: 2002109945

BowTie™ Press
A Division of BowTie Inc.
3 Burroughs
Irvine, California 92618
949-855-8822

Printed and Bound in Singapore
10 9 8 7 6 5 4 3 2

Foreword

For as long as there have been people, there have probably been pets. And for probably just as long, people have wondered—what goes on in the minds of our pets? How intelligent are they? What are their hopes, ambitions, and dreams? Are they even capable of having hopes, ambitions, and dreams? Are they happy? Do they like living in their yards, cages, tanks, or bowls? And most importantly, what do they really think about us? We can only imagine . . .

Leigh Rubin

"Ohhh, you meant to bring a *stool* sample."

A favorite of high-tech kittens—
virtual ball of yarn

leigh

THE ART
OF
CAMOUFLAGE
leigh

Mazes that even baffle rats.

Harold's lifelong dream of developing a successful circus act was never to be realized.

America's favorite feline soap opera.

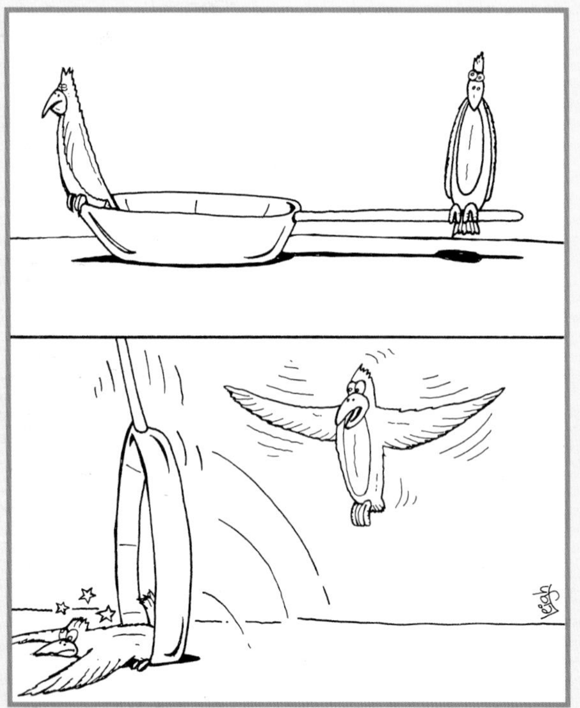

"Sorry old boy, I didn't mean to fly off the handle."

"Sorry, I won't be in, Boss. Either I caught some kind of bug or it was something I ate. Frankly, I'm not sure there's much of a difference."

"What's this world coming to? You can't even eat a worm without worrying that some psycho stuck a hook in it!"

"I'm afraid little Ronnie can't come out and play—he's come down with the plague."

Ralph felt that the sign was open to interpretation.

"This is pure heresy! Everybody knows that the world revolves around us!"

"You didn't want to be dissected?! What kind of excuse is that to fail science?!"

"I'm all for being environmentally responsible, but perhaps we should rethink our position on water conservation."

While it was a nice gesture for Ralph to have his mother-in-law over for dinner, she couldn't quite shake the uneasy feeling that his intentions were not entirely pure.

FIRST IT WAS DOG TAGS, THEN IT WAS LEASH LAWS. NOW THEY WANT TO PENALIZE US FOR HAVING CHILDREN! FRANKLY, I DIDN'T THINK THIS COULD HAPPEN IN AMERICA!
$50.00 FINE FOR LITTERING

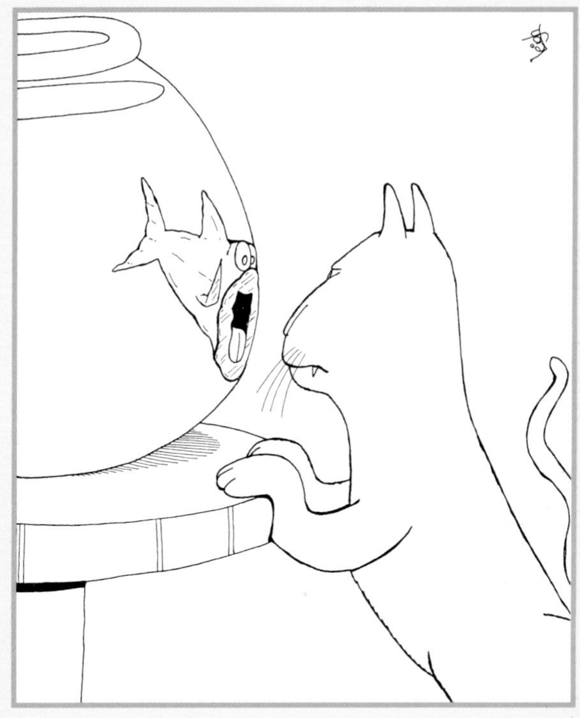

"If you don't mind, Ma, I'll skip dinner. Suddenly I've lost my appetite."

"Better call the paramedics—it looks like we've got ourselves a real jumper."

"Did you ever stop and think just how much our living conditions might improve if that thing wasn't purely decorative?"

GOSH! DID YOU EVER WONDER HOW UNSANITARY THIS MUST HAVE BEEN BEFORE INDOOR PLUMBING?
Leigh

YOU DON'T WANT THE CHICKEN. YOU DON'T WANT THE FISH. YOU DON'T WANT THE BEEF. YOU'RE SO FINICKY! WHAT IS IT THAT YOU WANT, KITTY?
FILET O' RAT
Leigh

"Yes, dear, I realize a peephole might seem a bit superfluous, but these days, you just can't be too careful."

Occupational hazards of an amphibian doctor.

"Wow! What an absolutely unbelievable catch by McElroy—Though, from the looks of it, he'll probably be out the rest of the season!"

Rat Scouts

"Nope, no sign of your kitten, ma'am. But to be absolutely certain, we'd better perform a CAT scan."

"Look, honey, you made the paper again!"

"Nah, I don't think computers will ever completely replace newspapers—it'd be too expensive to line our cage."

"Geesh! As if existing on a diet of insects isn't bad enough, now we're supposed to worry about whether or not they're loaded with pesticides!"

"Big deal, so it comes with a view! They *all* come with a view!"

OUT
OF
ORDER
leigh

"READY...
AIM..."
leigh

"It pains me to tell you this, Herb, but I'm afraid I can't see you anymore."

Diary of a Fish

Marcie's day of soliciting contributions for her local chapter of Zero Population Growth immediately got off to a bad start.

"OK, boy, let's try it again . . ."

"I'm in the mood for a little treat, son.
How'd you like some baskin' robins?"

"If you think life is dull now just imagine what it was like before our bowls were made of glass."

"Now, observe carefully as I demonstrate the 'two birds, one stone' theory."

Bird Home Improvement Centers

The tortoise and the hair loss

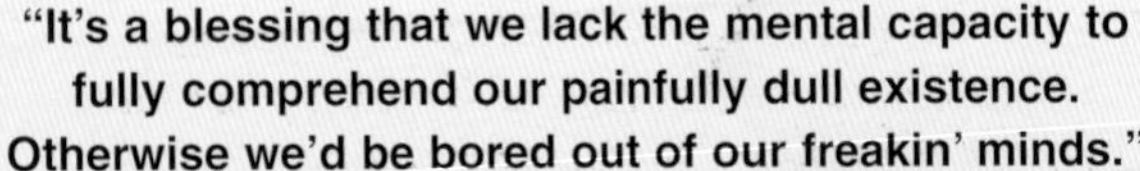
"It's a blessing that we lack the mental capacity to fully comprehend our painfully dull existence. Otherwise we'd be bored out of our freakin' minds."

"Next time, remind me to have the customers pay before they eat!"

"The good news is that Junior's finally housebroken. The bad news is that he still prefers the morning paper."

YESSIREE, THAT IS CERTAINLY ONE MIGHTY FINE BIRD DOG YA GOT THERE, BILLY BOB.
Leigh

MARRIAGE AND FAMILY COUNSELOR
THE PROBLEM IS THAT I ONLY WANT A LARGE FAMILY, BUT SHE WANTS A **REALLY** LARGE FAMILY!

Canary Islands
TRAVEL
Fly With Us!
leigh
CAT DREAM VACATIONS

HEY, CAN'T YOU WAIT UNTIL I'M FINISHED READING THE COMICS?
Leigh

WELL, IT'S AN INTERESTING THEORY. BUT IT WOULD TAKE SOME PRETTY SUBSTANTIAL EVIDENCE TO CONVINCE ME THAT AS A BREED WE'VE BEEN EXCESSIVELY INBRED.
Leigh

Leigh
THE GUEST SPEAKER EXPERIENCED GREAT DIFFICULTY DELIVERING HIS AFTER-DINNER SPEECH DUE TO A FROG IN HIS THROAT.

GLUG GLUG
GLUG GLUG
GLUG GLUG GLUG
GLUG GLUG
GLUG GLUG GLUG
GLUG GLUG GLUG
GLUG GLUG
GLUG GLUG
GLUG GLUG
GLUG GLUG
GLUG GLUG GLUG

IT'S FOOLPROOF, I TELL YOU. AS SOON AS THE CAT STARTS DRINKING I'LL PUSH THE LID DOWN AND YOU'LL JUMP ON THE LEVER.
leigh

leigh
I'M TIRED OF JUST WATCHING THE WORLD GO BY! I'M GOING TO GO OUT THERE AND EXPERIENCE **LIFE!**

leigh

“Well, congratulations, you got him to sing. Now let’s see if you can get him to *TALK*!”

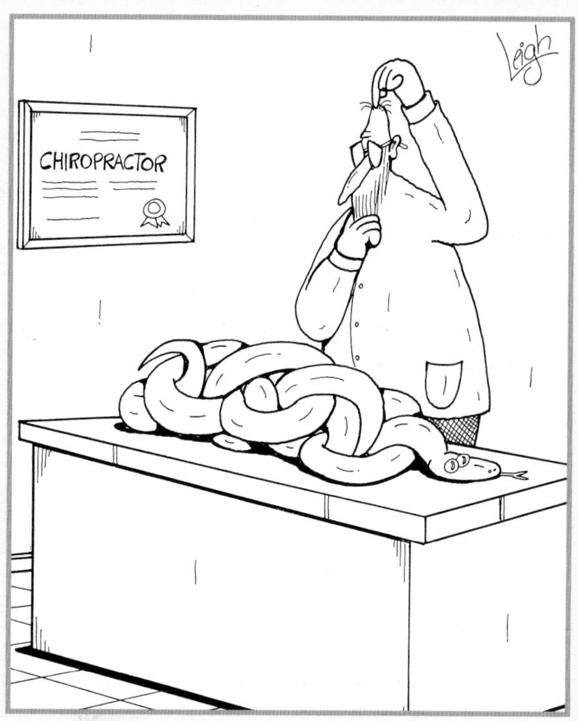

Dr. Thompson faces the most challenging spinal adjustment of his entire career.

"Hey c'mon, Sally . . . when are you gonna let me have a turn?!"

The Trials of Homing Pigeon Parenthood

"Why in the world did you buy another piece of exercise equipment when it's obvious you don't even use the one you have?!"

"Great. You know what this means? Overpriced food, small portions, and no doggy bags."

"I don't care what all the other kids are doing, you're *not* getting your lip pierced!"

"Just as I feared. We're being replaced by modern technology."

It took years of painstaking training, but eventually, Pierre taught his talking parrot to perform everything he knew.

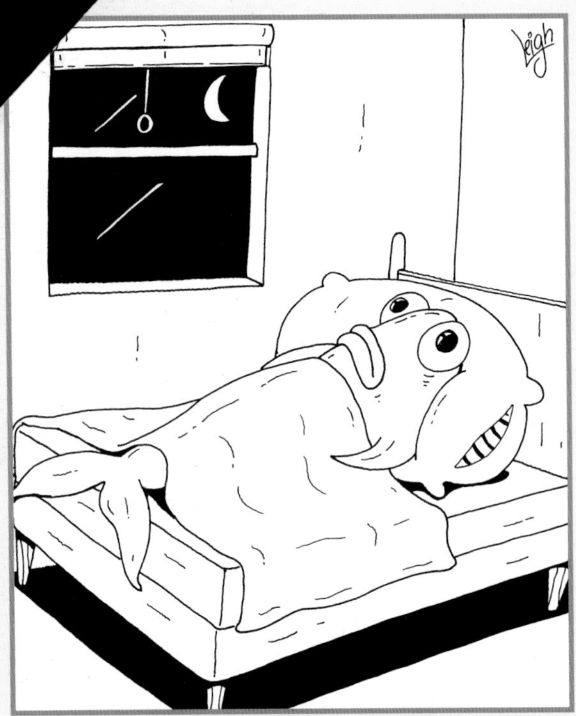

It wasn't insomnia that kept Leon wide awake night after night, just a simple lack of eyelids.

"Aw, for cryin' out loud, there goes the reception again! Junior! How many times have I told you not to gnaw on the cable?!"

One sign that indicates your cat is too finicky.

"Watch the birdie!"

Rover did his business on the carpet.

"There's been an escape, Deputy. Round up a posse. He couldn't have gotten very far!"

"I've been stuck here all day with the kids. The least you could do is to swoop down and pick us up some dinner on the way home!"

“There I was, swimming peacefully in the pond, when suddenly, some kid scoops me up and stuffs me in his pocket. The next thing I know, I’m dumped in with the laundry. Why, if that Maytag hadn’t been on the cold cycle I’d have been a goner!”

Despite a nearly obsessive daily exercise routine, Hazel found it nearly impossible to shed those last few grams.

"Boy, are you lucky your father's not here to see this. He'd break your neck—that is if you haven't already done it yourself."

"For the last time, Gramps, stop slobbering all over the windshield. The bugs are on the *outside*!"

"You're not going anywhere—this baby's *really* flooded!"

Because the plaintiffs were unable to positively identify their assailant, the farmer's wife was acquited.

"Tomorrow morning at 5:30 A.M. sharp, there'll be an early bird waiting outside this hole—that's where you come in."

"Gosh, the old house hasn't changed a bit. You've even kept my room just like it was when I lived here!"

Chameleon moms

"I'm telling you, Sylvia. Before we put up the fence I was a nervous wreck worrying that one of the kids might slip and fall out!"

Unable to cope with the yearly burden of delivering some thirty million eggs, he cracked and ended up an Easter basket case.

Cat burial plots

Newton discovers gravity—twice.

Reptile tanning salons

Goldfish adoption agencies

Sylvia regretted going to Phil's pad to see his bug collection.

"It is my understanding that you are seeking the meaning of your own existence, but unfortunately you don't exist."

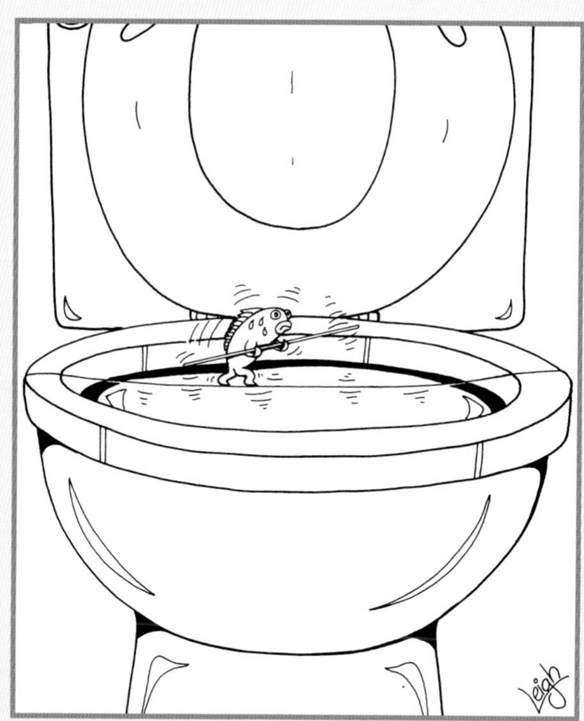

Goldfish thrill seekers

"Well, what are you waiting for, you stupid moron? Jump!"

"Of course I love you, Zelda. And nothing with the sole exception of 150 degree asphalt, will ever come between us."

"Looks like another depressingly wet day as usual."

How to tell you're in a very rough neighborhood.

Every afternoon Herb enjoyed a nice, relaxing catnap.